Contents

WHITE FISH AND CREOLE POTATO CASSEROLE

Prep Time: 15 mins - **Total Time:** 1 hr

SERVINGS PER RECIPE: 4

NUTRITIONAL VALUE

Calories 143.1 , Fat 1.1g , Cholesterol 38.0mg , Sodium 106.7mg , Carbohydrates 20.6g , Protein 13.5g

INGREDIENTS

- 2 medium sweet potatoes, sliced
- 4 C. spinach, chopped
- 1/2 onion, peeled and sliced thinly
- 8 small roma tomatoes, diced
- 1/2-3/4 lb white fish fillet
- 1 dash creole seasoning
- 3-5 garlic cloves, peeled

DIRECTIONS

Step 1

Before you do anything, preheat the oven to 450 F.

Step 2

Grease a Dutch oven with some olive oil. Lay in it onion slices followed by the white fish fillets. Season them with the Cajun seasoning.

Step 3

Top it with potatoes, garlic, onions, and tomatoes. Lay the spinach on top then season them with some salt and pepper.

Step 4

Place the pot in the oven and let them cook for 44 min. Serve your fish casserole warm.

Step 5

Enjoy.

OKRA JUMBO STEW

Prep Time: 10 mins - **Total Time:** 30 mins

SERVINGS PER RECIPE: 4

NUTRITIONAL VALUE

Calories 932.2 , Fat 44.5g , Cholesterol 372.4mg , Sodium 2426.1mg , Carbohydrates 25.7g , Protein 103.2g

INGREDIENTS

- 2 tbsp vegetable oil
- 1 lb turkey sausage, sliced
- 1/4 C. hot sauce
- 2 lbs chicken tenders, diced
- 1 lb medium raw shrimp, peeled and
- 1 medium yellow onion, sliced
- deveined
- 3 large garlic cloves, chopped
- 8 oz. frozen okra, defrosted
- 3 celery ribs, chopped
- 1/4 C. fresh flat-leaf parsley, chopped
- 1 green pepper, thin strips
- 4 scallions, green and white parts, thinly
- 1 red bell pepper, thin strips
- sliced
- 4 sprigs fresh thyme
- 2 C. chicken stock
- 1 C. tomato juice

DIRECTIONS

Step 1

Place a large pan over medium heat. Heat the oil in it.

Step 2

Cook in it the sausage for 4 min. Push it to one side of the pan. Cook the chicken tenders on the other side with a pinch of salt and pepper for 4 min.

Step 3

Add the onion with garlic, celery, bell peppers, thyme, a pinch of salt and pepper. Mix them all well and let them cook for 6 min.

Step 4

Stir in the stock, tomato sauce, and hot sauce. Cook them until they start boiling.

Step 5

Stir in the shrimp and okra. Put on the lid and let them cook for 6 min. fold the parsley and scallions into the stew then serve it hot.

Step 6

Enjoy.

SMOKED VENISON JERKY

Prep Time: 15 mins **- Total Time:** 24 hr 15 mins

SERVINGS PER RECIPE: 15

NUTRITIONAL VALUE

Calories 99.2 , Fat 4.3g , Cholesterol 48.4mg , Sodium 90.5mg , Carbohydrates 1.1g , Protein 13.2g

INGREDIENTS

- 2 lbs ground venison
- 1/4 C. liquid smoke
- 1/4 C. Cajun seasoning
- 1 tbsp black pepper

- 1/4 C. Worcestershire sauce

DIRECTIONS

Step 1

Get a large mixing bowl: Stir in it all the Ingredients. Spread the mix on the dehydrating trays.

Step 2

Dehydrate the jerky for 6 h 20 min on 156 degrees. Serve your jerky right away or store them sealing bags.

Step 3

Enjoy.

MIRACLE TUNA DIP

Prep Time: 5 mins **- Total Time:** 10 mins

SERVINGS PER RECIPE: 9

NUTRITIONAL VALUE

Calories 62.4 , Fat 4.0g , Cholesterol 17.2mg , Sodium 33.7mg , Carbohydrates 0.9g , Protein 5.5g

INGREDIENTS

- 1/3 C. cream cheese, softened
- 3 tbsp Miracle Whip
- 1 (6 1/2 oz.) cans tuna, drained and broken
- 1 tsp paprika
- into chunks
- 1/4 tsp black pepper
- 1/4 C. finely chopped bell pepper
- 1/4 tsp garlic powder
- 2 tbsp thinly sliced sweet onions
- 1/4 tsp ground red pepper

DIRECTIONS

Step 1

Get a small mixing bowl: Mix in it the cream cheese, Miracle Whip, paprika, black pepper, garlic powder, and red pepper until they become light and smooth.

Step 2

Fold the tuna, bell pepper, and onion into the mix. Place the dip in the fridge and let it sit for at least 4 h in the fridge.

Step 3

Serve your dip whenever you desire.

Step 4

Enjoy.

SWEET HONEY CHICKEN

Prep Time: 10 mins **- Total Time:** 1 hr 45 mins

SERVINGS PER RECIPE: 4

NUTRITIONAL VALUE

Calories 481 kcal, Fat 21.5 g, Carbohydrates 49.4g, Protein 22.8 g, Cholesterol 65 mg, Sodium 6378 mg

INGREDIENTS

- 3 C. cold water
- 1/2 tsp garlic salt
- 1/4 C. kosher salt
- 1/2 tsp onion salt
- 1/4 C. honey
- cayenne pepper to taste
- 4 boneless skinless chicken breast halves
- vegetable oil for frying
- 1/4 C. buttermilk
- 1 C. all-purpose flour

- 1 tsp black pepper

DIRECTIONS

Step 1

Get a bowl, combine: honey, water, and salt.

Step 2

Now place the chicken in the water (make sure the liquid covers the chicken).

Step 3

Place a covering of plastic wrap around the bowl and chill the mix in the fridge for 2 hrs.

Step 4

Now put your chicken in another bowl and cover it with buttermilk.

Step 5

Let the chicken stand for 30 mins in the milk.

Step 6

Add your veggie oil to a frying and pan and begin heating it to 350 degrees before doing anything else.

Step 7

Now get a 3rd bowl, mix: cayenne, flour, onion salt, garlic salt, and black pepper.

Step 8

Dredge your chicken in the dry mix then fry it for 13 mins per side in the hot oil **Step 9**

Enjoy.

AMERICAN DINNER ROLLS

Prep Time: 15 mins - **Total Time:** 35 mins

SERVINGS PER RECIPE: 4

NUTRITIONAL VALUE

Calories 202, Fat 11.1g, Cholesterol 26mg, Sodium 368mg, Carbohydrates 18.4g, Protein 6.4g

INGREDIENTS

- 1 C. Parmesan cheese, grated freshly
- 1 (1 lb.) frozen bread dough loaf, cut into 36 equal ½ C. butter, melted
- pieces

DIRECTIONS

Step 1

Grease 12 cups of a large-sized muffin tin.

Step 2

Divide grated cheese in prepared muffin cups evenly.

Step 3

In a bowl, add melted butter.

Step 4

With your hands, roll each piece of dough in a ball shape.

Step 5

Then dip the dough balls in melted butter completely.

Step 6

Place 3 balls in each muffin cup and gently, press down the balls in cheese.

Step 7

Cover the muffin cups with a light cloth. Keep in warm place for about 5-7 ours.

Step 8

Set your oven to 375 degrees F.

Step 9

Bake for about 20-25 minutes or till golden brown.

AUTHENTIC SOUTHERN CORN

Prep Time: 10 mins - **Total Time:** 20 mins

SERVINGS PER RECIPE: 6

NUTRITIONAL VALUE

Calories 359 kcal, Fat 22.7 g, Carbohydrates 38.2g, Protein 8 g, Cholesterol mg, Sodium 491 mg

INGREDIENTS

- 2 (15.25 oz.) cans whole kernel corn, drained
- 1 (8 oz.) package cream cheese
- 1/4 C. butter
- 10 jalapeno peppers, diced
- 1 tsp garlic salt

DIRECTIONS

Step 1

Cook the following for 15 mins, in a large, pot: garlic salt, corn, jalapenos, butter, and cream cheese.

Step 2

Stir the mix every 2 to 3 mins.

Step 3

Enjoy.

GOOD DAY CRAB BOIL

Prep Time: 30 mins - **Total Time:** 1 hr

SERVINGS PER RECIPE: 15

NUTRITIONAL VALUE

Calories 722 kcal, Fat 29.4 g, Carbohydrates 45.8g, Protein 67.6 g, Cholesterol 333 mg, Sodium 1576 mg

INGREDIENTS

- 1 tbsp seafood seasoning
- 5 lb. new potatoes
- 5 lb. whole crab, broken into pieces
- 3 (16 oz.) packages cooked turkey kielbasa
- 4 lb. fresh shrimp, peeled and deveined
- sausage, cut into 1 inch pieces
- 8 ears fresh corn, husks and silks removed

DIRECTIONS

Step 1

Heat a large pan of water over an outdoor cooker.

Step 2

Stir in the Old Bay Seasoning and bring to a boil.

Step 3

Stir in the potatoes and sausage and cook for about 10 minutes.

Step 4

Stir in the corn and crab and cook for about 5 minutes.

Step 5

Stir in the shrimp and cook for about 3-4 minutes.

Step 6

Drain the liquid from the pan and serve.

CREOLE SEASONING

Prep Time: 5 mins - **Total Time:** 5 mins

SERVINGS PER RECIPE: 20

NUTRITIONAL VALUE

Calories 16 kcal, Fat < 0.4 g, Carbohydrates < 3.4g, Protein 0.7 g, Cholesterol 0 mg, Sodium 1048 mg

INGREDIENTS

- 2 tbsps onion powder
- 2 tbsps garlic powder
- 1 tbsp white pepper
- 2 tbsps dried oregano
- 1 tbsp cayenne pepper
- 2 tbsps dried basil
- 5 tbsps paprika
- 1 tbsp dried thyme
- 3 tbsps salt
- 1 tbsp black pepper

DIRECTIONS

Step 1

Get a bowl, combine: salt, onion powder, paprika, garlic powder, cayenne, oregano, white pepper, thyme, black pepper, and basil.

Step 2

Stir the spices evenly then place them in a shaker or spice container.

Step 3

Enjoy.

CAJUN SEASONING

Prep Time: 5 mins **- Total Time:** 10 mins

SERVINGS PER RECIPE: 12

NUTRITIONAL VALUE

Calories 19.5 , Fat 0.5g , Cholesterol 0.0mg , Sodium 200.8mg , Carbohydrates 4.0g , Protein 0.9g

INGREDIENTS

- 5 tbsp paprika
- 1 tbsp oregano
- 2 tbsp garlic powder
- 1 tsp salt
- 1 tbsp black pepper
- 1 tsp chili powder
- 1 tbsp ground red pepper
- 1 tsp onion powder
- 1 tbsp white pepper
- 1 tbsp thyme

DIRECTIONS

Step 1

Get a small mixing bowl: Mix in it all the Ingredients. Place it in the storing jar then use it whenever your desire.

Step 2

Enjoy.

CAJUN CLAM CHOWDER

Prep Time: 5 mins **- Total Time:** 15 mins

SERVINGS PER RECIPE: 6

NUTRITIONAL VALUE

Calories 192.4 , Fat 10.2g , Cholesterol 60.3mg , Sodium 523.1mg , Carbohydrates 6.1g , Protein 18.6g

INGREDIENTS

- 1/4 C. vegetable oil
- 1/4 C. all-purpose flour
- 2 tbsp chopped fresh thyme
- 3-5 tsp Cajun seasoning
- 1 garlic clove, pressed
- 2 1/2 C. bottled clam juice
- 1 lb lump crabmeat
- 2 (14 1/2 oz.) cans diced tomatoes, in juice
- 1 (6 oz.) bags baby spinach leaves

DIRECTIONS

Step 1

Place a large pot over medium heat. Heat the oil in it. Add the flour and mix it well. Let it cook for 2 to 3 min until it becomes golden.

Step 2

Mix in it the Cajun seasoning with a pinch of salt. Stir in the clam juice with tomato. Cook them for 4 min.

Step 3

Stir in the spinach, thyme, and garlic. Let them cook for an extra 2 min.

Step 4

Stir in the crabmeat and cook the stew for an extra 2 minutes. Serve your chowder hot.

Step 5

Enjoy.

JULIA STREET CHOWDER

Prep Time: 10 mins **- Total Time:** 35 mins

SERVINGS PER RECIPE: 1

NUTRITIONAL VALUE

Calories 524.5 , Fat 19.4g , Cholesterol 286.4mg , Sodium 2620.9mg , Carbohydrates 42.0g , Protein 46.2g

INGREDIENTS

- 1 tbsp olive oil
- 2 tsps Cajun seasoning
- 1/2 lb medium shrimp, peeled, de-veined
- 2 tbsp all-purpose flour
- 1/2 C. chopped onion
- 2 tbsp water
- 1/2 C. chopped green pepper
- 1 cans diced tomatoes, undrained
- 2 C. frozen Hash Browns, chopped slightly
- 1 cans chicken broth

DIRECTIONS

Step 1

Place a pot over medium heat. Heat the oil in it. Cook in it the shrimp, onion and green pepper for 4 min.

Step 2

Stir in the Potatoes, broth and Cajun seasoning. Cook them until they start boiling. Lower the heat and let the soup cook for 24 min.

Step 3

Get a small mixing bowl: Combine in it the water with flour. Stir them into the soup followed by the tomato.

Step 4

Cook the soup for 6 min then serve it hot.

Step 5

Enjoy.

ROYAL STREET MEATBALL STEW

Prep Time: 45 mins - **Total Time:** 1 h 45 mins

SERVINGS PER RECIPE: 6

NUTRITIONAL VALUE

Calories 765.9 , Fat 55.7g , Cholesterol 167.7mg , Sodium 208.4mg , Carbohydrates 32.3g , Protein 33.3g

INGREDIENTS

- 3/4 C. vegetable oil
- 1 C. all-purpose flour
- 1 tbsp Worcestershire sauce
- 3 C. onions, finely chopped
- 1/2 C. fresh parsley, chopped
- 1 1/2 C. bell peppers, finely chopped
- 1/3 C. plain breadcrumbs
- 1 C. celery, finely chopped
- salt and cayenne pepper
- water or beef broth
- 1/4 C. green onion, chopped
- 4 garlic cloves, minced
- 2 lbs ground chuck
- 2 large eggs
- 1/4 C. milk

DIRECTIONS

Step 1

Place a large pot over medium heat. Heat the oil in it. Mix the flour into it and cook it until it becomes golden brown.

Step 2

Mix in it 2 C. of the chopped onion, 1 C. of the bell pepper and 1/2 C. of the celery. Cook them for 5 to 6 min.

Step 3

Pour enough broth or water in the pot to fill 2/3 of it. Cook the soup until it starts boiling. Lower the heat and let it cook.

Step 4

Get a large mixing bowl: Mix in it the ground chuck, remaining onions, bell pepper, and celery, 2 cloves of the minced garlic and eggs.

Step 5

Add the milk with Worcestershire sauce, 1/4 C. of the parsley, bread crumbs, and salt and cayenne pepper then mix them well.

Step 6

Shape the mix into bite size meatballs. Lower the meatballs into the pot and let them cook for 22 min without stirring them.

Step 7

Add the cayenne pepper, rest of the garlic, parsley, green onion and a pinch of salt. Cook the stew for an extra 6 min.

Step 8

Serve your stew hot with some rice.

Step 9

Enjoy.

BLACKENED POTATO CRUSTED SHRIMP

Prep Time: 15 mins - **Total Time:** 25 mins

SERVINGS PER RECIPE: 4

NUTRITIONAL VALUE

Calories 142.8 , Fat 7.9g , Cholesterol 143.0mg , Sodium 642.5mg , Carbohydrates 1.7g , Protein 15.5g

INGREDIENTS

- 1 lb jumbo shrimp, shelled and deveined
- 2 tbsp vegetable oil
- 1 tsp blackening seasoning
- 1 small lemon
- 2 C. frozen Hash Browns

DIRECTIONS

Step 1

Get a large mixing bowl: Toss in it the shrimp with Cajun blackening seasoning.

Step 2

Place a large pan over medium heat. Heat the oil in it. Press the potato hash into the shrimp then cook them in the hot oil for 4 to 5 min on each side.

Step 3

Squeeze over them some fresh lemon juice.

Step 4

Enjoy.

CAJUN VANILLA PIE

Prep Time: 25 mins - **Total Time:** 1 h 55 mins

SERVINGS PER RECIPE: 8

NUTRITIONAL VALUE

Calories 420.9 , Fat 14.7g , Cholesterol 89.5mg , Sodium 337.9mg , Carbohydrates 69.7g , Protein 4.6g

INGREDIENTS

- 3 medium sweet potatoes, boiled and
- mashed
- 1/2 C. chopped pecans
- 1/4 C. brown sugar
- 3/4 C. granulated sugar
- 2 tbsp sugar
- 2 large eggs
- 1 tbsp butter
- 3/4 C. dark corn syrup
- 1 tbsp pure vanilla extract
- 1 tbsp butter, melted
- 1 large egg
- 1/2 tsp salt
- 1 tbsp heavy cream
- ground cinnamon
- 1/4 tsp ground cinnamon
- 2 tsps pure vanilla extract
- 1 pinch nutmeg
- whipped cream
- 1 pinch ground allspice
- 1 9" unbaked pie shell

DIRECTIONS

Step 1

Before you do anything, preheat the oven to 300 F.

Step 2

Get a large mixing bowl: Beat in it the sweet potatoes, both sugars, butter, vanilla, egg, cinnamon, nutmeg, and allspice until they become smooth.

Step 3

Spoon the mix into the pie crust. Garnish it with the pecans.

Step 4

Get a mixing bowl: Mix in it the granulated sugar, eggs, corn syrup, melted butter, salt, cinnamon and vanilla.

Step 5

Sprinkle the mix over the pecan layer. Place the pie in the oven and let it cook for 1 h 32 min.

Step 6

Allow the pie to cool down completely then serve it with your favorite toppings.

Step 7

Enjoy.

FRENCH QUARTER GREEN BEANS

Prep Time: 30 mins - **Total Time:** 1 h 30 mins

SERVINGS PER RECIPE: 6

NUTRITIONAL VALUE

Calories 438.8 , Fat 29.9g , Cholesterol 85.7mg , Sodium 837.1mg , Carbohydrates 27.9g , Protein 18.1g

INGREDIENTS

- 4 slices thick-sliced turkey bacon, cut into
- 1/2 C. heavy cream
- pieces
- 1 1/2 C. grated white cheddar cheese
- 2 small onions, chopped
- 4 C. chicken broth
- 2 garlic cloves
- salt and pepper
- 3 lbs green beans

- 2 (6 oz.) cans fried onions
- 1/4 C. butter
- 1 pinch of grated nutmeg
- 1/2 C. all-purpose flour

DIRECTIONS

Step 1

Before you do anything, preheat the oven to 350 F.

Step 2

Place a Dutch oven over medium heat. Cook in it the bacon for 5 min. Stir into it the onion and cook them for 7 min.

Step 3

Stir in the garlic and cook them for 2 min. Place it aside.

Step 4

Stir in the green beans with enough broth or water to cover it in a large saucepan.

Step 5

Lower the heat put on the lid. Let the mix cook for 30 min. drain the beans and reserve the cooking liquid.

Step 6

Place a large pan over medium heat. Heat in it the butter until it melts. Sauté in it the rest of the onion with salt and nutmeg. Place it aside.

Step 7

Cook them for 7 min. Mix in the flour followed by the cream and the reserved bean cooking liquid. Cook it for 6 min until it mixture becomes thick.

Step 8

Add the cheese and green beans and cook them for few minutes until the cheese melts.

Step 9

Pour the mix into a glass casserole dish. Place it in the oven and let it cook for 26 min. spread the onion and bacon mix on top.

Step 10

Bake it for an extra 14 min. Serve it hot.

Step 11

Enjoy.

HOUMA POTATO POTS

Prep Time: 20 mins **- Total Time:** 1 h 50 mins

SERVINGS PER RECIPE: 2

NUTRITIONAL VALUE

Calories 642.4 , Fat 32.5g , Cholesterol 375.2mg , Sodium 1689.0mg , Carbohydrates 37.3g , Protein 49.4g

INGREDIENTS

- 1 lb jumbo shrimp, deveined
- 2 large baking potatoes
- 2 tbsp minced garlic
- 1 C. guacamole
- 1/2 C. sour cream
- 3 tbsp Cajun seasoning
- 1 C. shredded cheddar cheese

DIRECTIONS

Step 1

Before you do anything, preheat the grill.

Step 2

Place each potato in the middle of piece of foil and wrap it around it. Place it on the grill and let them cook until they become slightly soft.

Step 3

Toss the shrimp with Cajun seasoning and garlic in a shallow roasting pan. Place the pan over the grill on the indirect side of it.

Step 4

Let the shrimp cook for 12 min. Flip it and let cook for another 12 min.

Step 5

Once the shrimp and potato are done place them aside to lose heat for a while.

Step 6

Discard the foil sheets and slice them in half. Spoon some of the potato flesh to leave 1/4 of it only.

Step 7

Place 4 shrimp aside. Chop the remaining shrimp and place it in the potato shells followed by the cheese.

Step 8

Place each one of them in a foil packet. Place them over the grill and let them cook for an extra 12 min.

Step 9

Place the 4 shrimps in a small foil packet and grill them for 6 min.

Step 10

Once the time is up, top the shrimp layer with guacamole and sour cream. Garnish them with the whole remaining 4 shrimps. Serve them right away.

Step 11

Enjoy.

BAKED SOLE WITH CAULIFLOWER SALAD

Prep Time: 10 mins **- Total Time:** 40 mins

SERVINGS PER RECIPE: 2

NUTRITIONAL VALUE

Calories 744.6 , Fat 14.0g , Cholesterol 328.2mg , Sodium 1111.4mg , Carbohydrates 22.8g , Protein 129.0g

INGREDIENTS

- 8 sole fillets
- 1 green onion
- 3 C. French style green beans
- salt
- 3 C. cauliflower, florets
- pepper
- 1 tbsp butter
- Cajun seasoning
- 1/8 C. lemon juice

DIRECTIONS

Step 1

Before you do anything, preheat the oven to 350 F.

Step 2

Place the sole fillets on a greased baking pan. Drizzle over them the fresh lemon juice followed by the Cajun seasoning.

Step 3

Place the sole sheet in the oven and let it cool for 32 min.

Step 4

Place the cauliflower in a heatproof bowl. Cook it in the microwave for 9 min.

Step 5

Get a heatproof bowl: Stir in it the green beans with green onion. Cook them in the microwave for 9 min.

Step 6

Drain the coked veggies. Add to them the butter with a pinch of salt and pepper. Toss them to coat.

Step 7

Serve your baked sole with the veggies salad.

Step 8

Enjoy.

CREOLE COUNTRY HENS

Prep Time: 10 mins **- Total Time:** 24 h 10 mins

SERVINGS PER RECIPE: 4

NUTRITIONAL VALUE

Calories 1602.6 , Fat 107.1g , Cholesterol 756.2mg , Sodium 389.7mg , Carbohydrates 20.1g, Protein 129.3g

INGREDIENTS

- 4 oz. hot smoked beef sausage, chopped
- 1/2 C. long grain white rice
- 1/4 tsp dried thyme leaves
- 1 cans diced tomatoes
- 4 Cornish hens
- 1/2 C. sliced green onion
- 1 tbsp butter, melted
- 1/4 C. chopped green bell pepper

- 1 garlic clove, minced

DIRECTIONS

Step 1

Place a pot over medium heat. Cook in it the sausages for 8 min. add the rice and let them cook for 3 min.

Step 2

Stir in the tomatoes, onions, pepper, garlic and thyme. Cook them until they start boiling.

Put on the lid and let them cook for 22 min.

Step 3

Spoon the mix into the cavity of the hens. Place them in a greased roasting pan and coat them with butter, a pinch of salt and pepper.

Step 4

Place them in the oven and let them cook for 60 min. allow them to rest for 5 min then serve them warm.

Step 5

Enjoy.

LAKE CHARLES AVOCADO GLAZED KABOBS

Prep Time: 15 mins **- Total Time:** 25 mins

SERVINGS PER RECIPE: 2

NUTRITIONAL VALUE

Calories 525.3 , Fat 47.7g , Cholesterol 85.6mg , Sodium 482.4mg , Carbohydrates 18.0g , Protein 11.7g

INGREDIENTS

- 20 large uncooked prawns, peeled and
- 2 tbsp sour cream
- deveined
- 2 tbsp mayonnaise
- 2 tbsp Cajun seasoning
- 1 tsp Tabasco sauce
- 2 tsps ground cumin
- 1/2 tsp garlic powder
- 1 tsp dried oregano
- 1 tbsp fresh coriander, chopped
- 2 garlic cloves, crushed
- 1 tbsp lemon juice
- 50 ml olive oil
- 1 large avocado

DIRECTIONS

Step 1

Get a large mixing bowl: Stir in it the prawns with Cajun seasoning, oregano, cumin, garlic, olive oil, a pinch of salt and pepper.

Step 2

Place the mix in the fridge to sit for at least 30 min.

Step 3

Before you do anything, preheat the grill and grease it.

Step 4

Drain the prawns and thread them into skewers. Place them on the grill and cook them for 4 to 5 min on each side.

Step 5

Get a blender: Place in it all the avocado sauce Ingredients. Blend them smooth.

Step 6

Serve your skewers warm with the avocado sauce.

Step 7

Enjoy.

CAJUN PILAF

Prep Time: 10 mins **- Total Time:** 30 mins

SERVINGS PER RECIPE: 2

NUTRITIONAL VALUE

Calories 530.8 , Fat 5.9g , Cholesterol 127.8mg , Sodium 514.2mg , Carbohydrates 70.5g , Protein 45.0g

INGREDIENTS

- cooking spray
- 1 small brown onion, chopped
- 1/4 tsp ground turmeric
- 2 celery ribs, chopped
- 3/4 C. long-grain white rice
- 2 garlic cloves, crushed
- 2 C. chicken stock
- 1/4 tsp ground cinnamon
- 1/4 C. flat leaf parsley, chopped
- 2 cloves
- 360 g white fish fillets
- 2 tsps Cajun seasoning

DIRECTIONS

Step 1

Place a pot over medium heat. Heat the oil in it. Add the onion, celery and garlic. Let them cook for 6 min.

Step 2

Stir in the seasonings and cook them for 1 min. Stir in the rice and cook them for an extra 2 min.

Step 3

Pour in the broth and cook them until they start boiling. Lower the heat and put on the lid. Cook the pilaf for 22 min.

Step 4

Fold the parsley into the pilaf.

Step 5

Place a large pan over medium heat. Heat a splash of oil in it.

Step 6

Season the fish fillets with Cajun spice, a pinch of salt and pepper. Cook them in the hot oil for 4 to 6 min on each side.

Step 7

Serve your fish fillets warm with the pilaf.

Step 8

Enjoy.

SOUTHERN LUNCH BOX (SPICY CORN SALAD)

Prep Time: 10 mins **- Total Time:** 8 h

SERVINGS PER RECIPE: 6

NUTRITIONAL VALUE

Calories 269.9 , Fat 20.7g , Cholesterol 1.2mg , Sodium 331.2mg , Carbohydrates 21.8g , Protein 3.2g

INGREDIENTS

- 17 1/2 oz. cook frozen kernel corn
- 1/4 C. wine vinegar
- 1 green bell pepper, diced
- 1 tsp creole mustard
- 1 red bell pepper, diced
- 1 tbsp dried basil leaves
- 1 C. hot pickled okra or 6 green onions
- 2 tbsp mayonnaise
- 1/2 C. parsley, minced
- 1/2 tsp black pepper
- 1 C. cherry tomatoes, halved
- 1/2 tsp Tabasco sauce
- Tabasco:
- salt
- 1 tsp sugar
- 1/2 C. olive oil

DIRECTIONS

Step 1

Get a large mixing bowl: Stir in it all the salad Ingredients.

Step 2

Get a small mixing bowl: Whisk in it the sauce Ingredients except of the oil.

Step 3

Add to it the olive oil in a steady stream while whisking it all the time. Drizzle the sauce over the salad.

Step 4

Place it in the fridge for an overnight then serve it.

Step 5

Enjoy.

CREOLE SEAFOOD FILLETS

Prep Time: 5 mins - **Total Time:** 15 mins

SERVINGS PER RECIPE: 2

NUTRITIONAL VALUE

Calories 435.4 , Fat 3.9g , Cholesterol 198.1mg , Sodium 544.6mg , Carbohydrates 10.2g , Protein 84.3g

INGREDIENTS

- 4 fish fillets
- butter-flavored cooking spray
- 2 tsps Cajun seasoning
- 1/4 C. seasoned breadcrumbs
- salt and pepper

DIRECTIONS

Step 1

Before you do anything, preheat the oven to 400 F.

Step 2

Place the fish fillets on a lined up baking sheet. Grease them with a cooking spray.

Step 3

Season them with the Cajun spice then top them with the bread crumbs.

Step 4

Place the fish pan in the oven. Cook it in the oven for 4 to 6 min. Serve it warm.

Step 5

Enjoy.

CREOLE ALFREDO

Prep Time: 5 mins **- Total Time:** 4 h 5 mins

SERVINGS PER RECIPE: 4

NUTRITIONAL VALUE

Calories 763.0 , Fat 48.6g , Cholesterol 227.6mg , Sodium 2723.5mg , Carbohydrates 14.8g , Protein 64.6g

INGREDIENTS

- 1 1/2-2 lbs boneless skinless chicken
- 1-2 tbsp Cajun seasoning
- garlic soup mix
- 1/4 tsp lemon pepper
- 8 oz. cream cheese
- canned mushroom
- 1 cans cream of chicken soup
- 8 oz. parmesan cheese
- 1 cans cream of mushroom soup
- linguine
- 1 cans water
- 2 chicken bouillon cubes

DIRECTIONS

Step 1

Stir the chicken with soup mix, cream cheese, mushroom soup, water, bouillon cubes, Cajun seasoning, lemon pepper, some canned mushroom, a pinch of salt and pepper.

Step 2

In a greased slow cooker. Put on the lid and let them cook for 4 h on low.

Step 3

Stir in the cheese until it melts. Serve your Alfredo sauce with some pasta.

Step 4

Enjoy.

CREOLE RUMP ROLLS

Prep Time: 10 mins - **Total Time:** 35 mins

SERVINGS PER RECIPE: 4

NUTRITIONAL VALUE

Calories 566.6 , Fat 15.4g , Cholesterol 76.2mg , Sodium 759.1mg , Carbohydrates 67.0g , Protein 38.1g

INGREDIENTS

- 500 g beef rump, sliced
- 1 yellow onion, sliced
- 3 medium tomatoes, wedges
- 1 red capsicum, sliced
- 1 French baguette
- 2 tbsp Cajun seasoning
- lettuce leaf

DIRECTIONS

Step 1

Place a large pan over medium heat. Heat the oil in it. Cook in it the beef for 8 min. Drain it and place it aside.

Step 2

Sauté in it the onion with capsicum and seasoning for 5 min in the same pan.

Step 3

Stir in the tomato wedges and cook them for 16 min over low heat. Add the browned beef to the pan.

Step 4

Slice the baguette open and lay in it the lettuce leaves. Spoon over it the beef mix. Serve it with your favorite toppings.

Step 5

Enjoy.

LEMON CREOLE CHICKEN

Prep Time: 10 mins **- Total Time:** 50 mins

SERVINGS PER RECIPE: 6

NUTRITIONAL VALUE

Calories 203.9 , Fat 13.8g , Cholesterol 69.0mg , Sodium 313.0mg , Carbohydrates 1.9g , Protein 17.2g

INGREDIENTS

- 1/2 C. lemon juice
- 3 tbsp Cajun seasoning
- 1/4 C. hot pepper sauce
- 2 lbs chicken

DIRECTIONS

Step 1

Before you do anything, preheat the oven to 350 F.

Step 2

Stir all the Ingredients in a greased baking dish.

Step 3

Place it in the oven and let it cook for 48 min. serve your chicken casserole warm.

Step 4

Enjoy.

HOMEMADE SPICY MUSTARD

Prep Time: 15 mins - **Total Time:** 15 mins

SERVINGS PER RECIPE: 1

NUTRITIONAL VALUE

Calories 851.0 , Fat 43.4g , Cholesterol 0.0mg , Sodium 38.9mg , Carbohydrates 93.4g , Protein 34.3g

INGREDIENTS

- 2 oz. dry mustard
- 1 tbsp flour
- 1 tsp cumin
- 3 tbsp malt vinegar
- 1 tsp thyme
- 1 tbsp honey
- 1 tsp black pepper
- 1 clove garlic, chopped
- 1 tsp paprika
- 1 tbsp hot pepper flakes

DIRECTIONS

Step 1

Get a mixing bowl: Stir in it the flour with mustard. Add to it 1/4 C. of cold water while mixing them all the time.

Step 2

Let the mustard sauce sit for 16 min. add the rest of the Ingredients and mix them well. Serve your sauce whenever you desire.

Step 3

Enjoy.

CREOLE PIZZA

Prep Time: 30 mins - **Total Time:** 1 h

SERVINGS PER RECIPE: 4

NUTRITIONAL VALUE

Calories 611.9 , Fat 37.6g , Cholesterol 115.5mg , Sodium 1530.6mg , Carbohydrates 33.1g , Protein 37.2g

INGREDIENTS

- 1 large pizza crusts
- 1 tbsp brown mustard
- 1/2 lb beef sausage, cooked, crumbled
- 1 tbsp chopped fresh ginger
- 2 chicken breasts, cooked, strips
- 2 tsps brown sugar
- 1 small zucchini, sliced
- 2 tsps Worcestershire sauce
- 1 red bell pepper, diced
- 2 tsps cumin
- 1/2 C. chopped onion
- 2 tsps other Cajun seasoning
- 2 cloves chopped garlic
- 1/2 tsp oregano
- 1 cans tomato sauce
- 1 dash hot sauce, to taste
- 1 cans diced tomatoes
- 8 oz. grated cheese

DIRECTIONS

Step 1

Before you do anything, preheat the oven to 350 F.

Step 2

Get a food processor: Combine in it the onions, tomato sauce, tomatoes, brown sugar, garlic, ginger, and all the seasonings.

Step 3

Pulse them several times until they become puréed to make the sauce.

Step 4

Transfer the sauce to a heavy saucepan. Let it cook for 35 min.

Step 5

Place the pizza crust on a lined up baking sheet. Top it wit half of the sauce followed by the zucchini slices and chicken.

Step 6

Top them with the sausage and bell peppers. Drizzle the remaining sauce on top with cheese.

Step 7

Place the pizza in the oven and let it cook for 16 min. serve it hot.

Step 8

Enjoy.

CREOLE SHRIMP TORTILLAS

Prep Time: 30 mins - **Total Time:** 40 mins

SERVINGS PER RECIPE: 8

NUTRITIONAL VALUE

Calories 306.6 , Fat 6.9g , Cholesterol 86.4mg , Sodium 469.2mg , Carbohydrates 42.1g , Protein 17.3g

INGREDIENTS

- 1/2 C. uncooked rice
- 1 tbsp olive oil
- 2 tsps Cajun seasoning
- 1 lb uncooked medium shrimp, peeled and
- 1 C. tomato sauce
- deveined

- 8 8-inch flour tortillas, warmed
- 1 small red onion, chopped
- 1 tbsp minced garlic

DIRECTIONS

Step 1

Cook the rice by following the instructions on the package.

Step 2

Place a large pan over medium heat. Heat the oil in it. Cook in it the shrimp, onion, garlic, and Cajun seasoning for 4 min.

Step 3

Mix in it the pasta sauce with cooked rice. Divide the mix between the tortillas and wrap them. Serve them right away.

Step 4

Enjoy.

CREOLE ICE CREAM

Prep Time: 3 hr - **Total Time:** 6 hr

SERVINGS PER RECIPE: 1 CARTON

NUTRITIONAL VALUE

Calories 3547.7 , Fat 269.6g , Cholesterol 1669.5mg , Sodium 608.2mg , Carbohydrates 261.3g , Protein 40.2g

INGREDIENTS

- 2 1/2 C. heavy cream
- 1/2 tsp cayenne pepper
- 1 C. whole milk
- 1 1/2 tbsp dried rosemary
- 3/4 C. dark brown sugar

- 1/4 C. pecans, lightly chopped
- 5 egg yolks
- 1 C. sweet potato puree, canned
- 1/4 tsp ground nutmeg
- 3/4 tsp ground cinnamon

DIRECTIONS

Step 1

Place a heavy saucepan over medium heat. Stir in it the cream, milk, and brown sugar until they become hot.

Step 2

Get a mixing bowl: Beat in it the eggs while adding 1 C. hot cream mix gradually. Stir the mix into the saucepan gradually while mixing all the time.

Step 3

Let it cook over medium heat while stirring all the time until it becomes slightly thick for 7 min.

Step 4

Once the again, pour the mix into a large mixing bowl. Add to it the sweet potato puree, nutmeg, cinnamon, cayenne pepper and rosemary. Mix them well.

Step 5

Cover the bowl with a plastic wrap and place it in the fridge for 2 h 30 min.

Step 6

Once the time is up, prepare the ice cream by following the manufacturer's instructions. Serve it with your favorite toppings.

Step 7

Enjoy.

CAJUN SAUSAGE KABOBS

Prep Time: 10 mins - **Total Time:** 25 mins

SERVINGS PER RECIPE: 4

NUTRITIONAL VALUE

Calories 333.5 , Fat 23.6g , Cholesterol 48.8mg , Sodium 1038.6mg , Carbohydrates 12.3g , Protein 17.7g

INGREDIENTS

- 1 beef sausages, sliced
- 1 green bell pepper, chopped
- 1 onion, diced
- 1 red bell pepper, chopped
- 1 tbsp Cajun seasoning
- 1 yellow bell pepper, chopped
- skewer

DIRECTIONS

Step 1

Before you do anything, preheat the grill and grease it.

Step 2

Thread the sausage slices with bell peppers and onion into the skewers while alternating between them.

Step 3

Season them with the Cajun seasoning, a pinch of salt and pepper. Cook the kabobs on the grill for 16 min or until they are done.

Step 4

Serve your kabobs with your favorite sauce.

Step 5

Enjoy.

CREOLE SHRIMP BITES

Prep Time: 45 mins **- Total Time:** 1 hr 4 mins

SERVINGS PER RECIPE: 1

NUTRITIONAL VALUE

Calories 62.6 , Fat 2.1g , Cholesterol 30.6mg , Sodium 186.2mg , Carbohydrates 7.3g , Protein 3.2g

INGREDIENTS

- 2 tbsp parsley, minced
- 1/2 lb shrimp, cooked
- 2 tbsp green onions, minced
- 2 eggs
- 2 tbsp butter
- 2 C. breadcrumbs
- 2 tbsp flour
- oil, for frying
- 1/2 C. milk
- 1/2 tsp salt
- 1/4 tsp hot pepper sauce

DIRECTIONS

Step 1

Place a saucepan over medium heat. Heat in it the butter. Add the green onions with parsley and cook them for 1 min.

Step 2

Add the flour and mix them well. Pour in the milk with hot sauce and a pinch of salt. Whisk them until they become smooth.

Step 3

Let them cook until they become thick. Turn off the heat and fold the shrimp into the mix.

Step 4

Allow the mix to cool down for a while then shape it into bite size balls.

Step 5

Whisk the eggs in a shallow bowl. Lower in it the shrimp balls then coat them with the bread crumbs, dip them again in the eggs and roll them in the breadcrumbs.

Step 6

Place them on a lined up baking sheet. Place the shrimp balls in the fridge and let them sit for 32 min.

Step 7

Place a large skillet over medium heat. Heat 1/4 to 1/2 inch of oil in it. Add the shrimp balls and cook them for 4 min until they become golden brown.

Step 8

Drain the shrimp balls then serve them with your favorite dip.

Step 9

Enjoy.

CAJUN TORTILLAS PAN

Prep Time: 20 mins - **Total Time:** 50 mins

SERVINGS PER RECIPE: 4

NUTRITIONAL VALUE

Calories 407.5 , Fat 18.1g , Cholesterol 73.4mg , Sodium 1131.2mg , Carbohydrates 36.7g , Protein 24.4g

INGREDIENTS

- 2 tbsp butter
- 2 C. cooked chicken, cubes

- 1/2 C. green bell pepper, chopped
- 6 flour tortillas, chopped
- 1/2 C. onion, chopped
- 1 1/2 C. shredded cheddar cheese
- 2 jalapeno peppers, chopped
- sour cream
- 4 oz. green chilies, chopped
- green onion
- 10 oz. condensed cream of chicken soup
- sliced avocado
- 10 oz. Rotel tomatoes & chilies

DIRECTIONS

Step 1

Before you do anything, preheat the oven to 325 F.

Step 2

Place a pot over medium heat. Heat in it the butter. Sauté in it the onion with pepper and jalapenos for 6 min.

Step 3

Stir in the green chiles, soup, Rotel tomatoes, and chicken.

Step 4

Lay 1/3 of the tortillas in a greased baking dish. Spread over it 1/3 of the chicken mix followed by 1/3 of the cheese.

Step 5

Repeat the process to make an extra 2 layers. Place the pan in the oven and let it cook for 35 min. serve it hot.

Step 6

Enjoy.

CREOLE SUMMER WATERMELON RELISH

Prep Time: 30 mins **- Total Time:** 55 mins

SERVINGS PER RECIPE: 40

NUTRITIONAL VALUE

Calories 25.0 , Fat 0.0g , Cholesterol 0.0mg , Sodium 175.8mg , Carbohydrates 5.7g , Protein 0.1g

INGREDIENTS

- 5 C. watermelon rind, diced
- 1 large onion, diced
- 1 tbsp pickling salt
- 1 red bell pepper, diced
- 1/2 tsp mustard, seed
- 1 green bell pepper, diced
- 1 bay leaf
- 1-2 fresh jalapeno pepper, sliced
- 1 tsp celery seed
- 1 C. sugar
- 1 tsp peppercorns
- 2 C. vinegar
- 1 tsp pepper, flakes

DIRECTIONS

Step 1

Get a large mixing bowl: Stir in it the onion with rind, peppers, and salt. Pour over them enough cold water to cover them.

Step 2

Place the bowl in the fridge and let it sit for an overnight.

Step 3

Get a large pot. Stir in it the sugar with vinegar, mustard, bay leaf, celery seed, peppercorns, and pepper flakes.

Step 4

Cook them over medium heat until they start boiling. Drain the rind and onion mix then stir it into the pot.

Step 5

Cook them until they start boiling again. Lower the heat and bring to a simmer.

Step 6

Spoon the mix into sterilized jars leaving 1/2 of space empty in each jar. Seal the jars and place them in some hot water for 12 min.

Step 7

Let them sit for at least 1 week before serving it.

Step 8

Enjoy.

CREOLE STUFFED PEPPERS

Prep Time: 45 mins **- Total Time:** 1 h 45 mins

SERVINGS PER RECIPE: 6

NUTRITIONAL VALUE

Calories 636.9 , Fat 32.2g , Cholesterol 105.8mg , Sodium 1325.7mg , Carbohydrates 54.6g , Protein 32.1g

INGREDIENTS

- 6-10 large bell peppers, tops and insides
- 1 medium bell pepper, chopped
- removed
- 1-2 tbsp minced garlic

- 4 C. cooked rice
- Cajun seasoning
- 24-32 oz. tomato sauce
- 1 lb ground beef
- 1 cans diced tomatoes & chilies
- 1 lb ground turkey sausage
- 1 large onion, chopped

DIRECTIONS

Step 1

Before you do anything, preheat the oven to 350 F.

Step 2

Place a large pan over medium heat. Cook in it the ground beef and ground sausage for 10 min. discard the excess grease.

Step 3

Stir in the seasonings, veggies, diced tomatoes, and tomato sauce. Cook them until the veggies are soft. Drain 2 C. of sauce from the mix and place it aside.

Step 4

Stir in the rice into the pan and turn off the heat to make the filling. Spoon the mix into the bell peppers.

Step 5

Place them in a greased casserole dish. Pour the reserve sauce all over it. Cook it in the oven for 60 min.

Step 6

Serve your stuffed peppers warm.

Step 7

Enjoy.

CAJUN TEX GUMBO

Prep Time: 40 mins **- Total Time:** 1 h 25 mins

SERVINGS PER RECIPE: 6

NUTRITIONAL VALUE

Calories 1201.9 , Fat 76.6g , Cholesterol 167.2mg , Sodium 1645.3mg , Carbohydrates 69.0g, Protein 55.2g

INGREDIENTS

- 1/4 C. all-purpose flour
- 1 tsp salt
- 1 C. lard
- 1/2 tsp black pepper
- 2 C. chopped onions
- 1/4 tsp cayenne
- 1 1/2 C. chopped green bell peppers
- 1 tsp paprika
- 1 1/2 C. chopped celery
- 1/2 tsp onion powder
- 2 quarts chicken stock
- 1/2 tsp garlic powder
- 3/4 lb beef sausage, cubed
- 6 chicken breasts, cubed
- 2 garlic cloves, minced
- 1/4 C. vegetable oil
- 3 C. cooked rice
- 1 C. all-purpose flour

DIRECTIONS

Step 1

Get a large mixing bowl: Toss in it the spices with chicken and 1/4 C. of flour.

Step 2

Place a large pan over medium heat. Heat the oil in it. Add the chicken in batches and coo them for 5 min per batch.

Step 3

Place a pot over medium heat. Melt the lard in it. Add the flour and mix it well then cook it until it becomes golden brown.

Step 4

Add the veggies and mix them well. Add to it the stock gradually while mixing them all the time.

Step 5

Cook them until they start boiling. Stir in the chicken, sausage, and garlic. Lower the heat and let the stew cook for 60 min.

Step 6

Adjust the seasoning of your gumbo then serve it warm.

Step 7

Enjoy.

QUICK CAJUN GUMBO

Prep Time: 1 hr **- Total Time:** 1 h 35 mins

SERVINGS PER RECIPE: 8

NUTRITIONAL VALUE

Calories 475.9 , Fat 24.9g , Cholesterol 77.2mg , Sodium 963.7mg , Carbohydrates 39.4g , Protein 21.2g

INGREDIENTS

- 1 box Zatarians gumbo base mix
- 2 C. long grain white rice
- 1 lb chicken
- 1/2 tbsp salt

- 1 lb smoked sausage
- 1 boxes sliced frozen okra, defrosted

DIRECTIONS

Step 1

Cook the rice by following the instructions on the package.

Step 2

Prepare the gumbo mix by following the instructions on the package.

Step 3

Pour the mix into a large pot over high heat. Cook it until it starts boiling while stirring it all the time.

Step 4

Stir in the meat and cook them until they start boiling again. Lower the heat and let the stew coo for 30 min while stirring it from time to time.

Step 5

Add the okra and cook them until they start boiling again. Serve your gumbo with white rice.

Step 6

Enjoy.

CREOLE CRAB CAKES

Prep Time: 30 mins **- Total Time:** 40 mins

SERVINGS PER RECIPE: 8

NUTRITIONAL VALUE

Calories 173.2 , Fat 6.1g , Cholesterol 115.6mg , Sodium 378.7mg , Carbohydrates 17.3g , Protein 13.2g

INGREDIENTS

- 2 roasted red peppers
- 1/2 C. fat-free mayonnaise
- 1 tbsp lemon juice
- 1/4-1/2 tsp cayenne pepper
- 1 tsp Cajun seasoning
- 1/2 tsp seasoning salt
- 1/2 tsp crab boil seasoning
- 3 tsps olive oil, divided
- 2 tsps Worcestershire sauce
- 1/2 onion, chopped
- 1/2 tsp mustard powder
- 1 stalk celery, chopped
- 1/4 tsp crushed celery seed
- 2 eggs, beaten
- 1/2 tsp ground paprika
- 2 tbsp ground walnuts
- 1 lb crawfish meat or 1 lb crabmeat
- 2 tbsp chopped fresh parsley
- 1/2-1 tsp hot pepper sauce
- 2 tbsp fat-free mayonnaise
- 1 C. whole wheat breadcrumbs

DIRECTIONS

Step 1

Get a food processor: Place in it the roasted peppers then process them until they become smooth.

Step 2

Pour in the mayonnaise and spices then blend them smooth to make the sauce. Place it in the fridge.

Step 3

Get a large mixing bowl: Combine in it all the Ingredients except for the bread crumbs. Shape the mix into 8 cakes then roll them in the breadcrumbs.

Step 4

Place a large pan over medium heat. Heat 2 tsps of olive oil. Cook in it the fish cakes for 3 to 4 min on each side.

Step 5

Serve your fish cakes warm with the pepper sauce.

Step 6

Enjoy.

BATON ROUGE CABBAGE STEW

Prep Time: 20 mins **- Total Time:** 35 mins

SERVINGS PER RECIPE: 12

NUTRITIONAL VALUE

Calories 111.9 , Fat 1.8g , Cholesterol 0.0mg , Sodium 701.8mg , Carbohydrates 22.3g , Protein 5.1g

INGREDIENTS

- 26 oz. pasta sauce
- salt and pepper
- 26 oz. extra mild salsa
- 8 oz. water or 8 oz. chicken stock
- 1 lb ground meat
- 2 large heads of cabbage

DIRECTIONS

Step 1

Bring a large salted pot of water to a boil. Core the cabbage and slice it into 1/2 inch thick slices.

Step 2

Cook them in the hot water for 3 to 4 min until they wilt.

Step 3

Place a pot over medium heat. Cook in it the meat for 8 min. Discard the excess grease. Rinse the cooked meat and drain it.

Step 4

Stir the cooked meat back in the pot with sauce, and salsa to wilted cabbage. Let it cook for 8 min.

Step 5

Serve your un-rolled cabbage stew warm.

Step 6

Enjoy.

SPICY MAYO SALAD

Prep Time: 10 mins **- Total Time:** 10 mins

SERVINGS PER RECIPE: 8

NUTRITIONAL VALUE

Calories 404.0 , Fat 22.3g , Cholesterol 7.6mg , Sodium 746.6mg , Carbohydrates 50.7g , Protein 5.2g

INGREDIENTS

- 3 cans corn, drained
- 2 C. shredded cheddar cheese
- 1 (11 1/2 oz.) bag Fritos corn chips
- 1 small purple onion, diced
- lots cracked black pepper
- 1 medium bell pepper, sliced
- 1 C. Hellmann's mayonnaise

DIRECTIONS

Step 1

Get a large mixing bowl: Stir in it the corn with cheese, onion, pepper, and mayonnaise.

Step 2

Place the salad in the fridge for few hours.

Step 3

Top the salad with the Fritos chips.

Step 4

Enjoy.

CREOLE SPRING ROLLS

Prep Time: 30 mins **- Total Time:** 40 mins

SERVINGS PER RECIPE: 10

NUTRITIONAL VALUE

Calories 361.5 , Fat 14.1g , Cholesterol 29.1mg , Sodium 630.0mg , Carbohydrates 43.6g , Protein 15.8g

INGREDIENTS

- 1/2 lb beef sausage, diced
- 1 ear corn, roasted
- 6 cloves garlic, minced
- 1 roasted red bell pepper
- 1 medium onion, minced
- 1 pinch cumin
- 1 cans black beans
- 1 pinch chili powder
- 1 avocado, diced
- salt and pepper
- 1/4 lb cheddar cheese, grated
- 15-20 eggroll wraps
- 2 tbsp fresh cilantro, chopped
- oil

DIRECTIONS

Step 1

Place a large pan over medium heat. Cook in it the sausage for 5 min. add the onion with garlic and cook them for 10 min to make the filling.

Step 2

Turn off the heat and spoon the mix into a mixing bowl to cool down.

Step 3

Lay a wrapper on a working surface with the pointed corner facing towards you. Brush its edges with some water.

Step 4

Place 3 tbsp of the filling in the middle of the wrapper then pull the pointed corner on top of it and press it to seal it.

Step 5

Brush the right and left corner over the filling and press them to seal them.

Step 6

Repeat the process with the remaining Ingredients.

Step 7

Place a large pan over medium heat. Heat in it 1 inch of oil. Cook in it the rolls in the batches until they become golden brown.

Step 8

Serve your crunchy rolls with your favorite sauce.

Step 9

Enjoy.

SHREVEPORT STEW

Prep Time: 20 mins **- Total Time:** 1 h 20 mins

SERVINGS PER RECIPE: 8

NUTRITIONAL VALUE

Calories 431.4 , Fat 18.3g , Cholesterol 199.6mg , Sodium 1415.0mg , Carbohydrates 21.5g , Protein 44.9g

INGREDIENTS

- 1 tsp olive oil
- 1 lb Italian turkey sausage
- 1 large onion, chopped
- 1 lb white fish fillet, chunks
- 1 tbsp basil leaves, crushed
- 1 lb sea scallops
- 1 tbsp oregano leaves, crushed
- 1 lb shrimp
- 2-3 cloves garlic, crushed
- 2 red bell peppers, chopped
- 4 cans diced tomatoes
- 2 stalks celery, chopped

DIRECTIONS

Step 1

Place a Dutch oven over medium heat. Cook in it the sausage for 8 min.

Step 2

Stir in the Basil, oregano and Garlic, onion, celery& pepper. Cook them for 22 min.

Step 3

Stir in the tomato and let them cook for an extra 22 min. Fold the seafood into the mix and let them cook for 6 to 8 min until they are done.

Step 4

Serve your stew hot with some pasta.

Step 5

Enjoy.

CREOLE FRIED CRABS

Prep Time: 15 mins **- Total Time:** 45 mins

SERVINGS PER RECIPE: 4

NUTRITIONAL VALUE

Calories 360.5 , Fat 16.2g , Cholesterol 61.0mg , Sodium 1469.2mg , Carbohydrates 27.0g , Protein 26.0g

INGREDIENTS

- 3 tsps canola oil, divided
- 1 small onion, finely diced
- 1/2 tsp grated lemon zest
- 1/2 C. finely diced green bell pepper
- 1/4 C. mayonnaise
- 1/2 C. frozen corn kernels, thawed
- 2 tbsp sour cream
- 1 1/2 tsps Cajun seasoning, divided
- 2 scallions, chopped
- 1 lb pasteurized crabmeat
- 2 tsps capers
- 1 large egg white
- 1 tbsp Dijon mustard
- 3/4 C. plain breadcrumbs
- 1 tbsp sweet relish
- 1/4 C. mayonnaise
- 1/4 tsp ground pepper

DIRECTIONS

Step 1

Before you do anything, preheat the oven to 425 F.

Step 2

Place a large pan over medium heat. Heat in it 1 tsp of oil. Sauté in it the onion, bell pepper, corn and 1 tsp Cajun seasoning for 5 mins.

Step 3

Drain them and transfer them to a mixing bowl. Let it sit for 6 min. Mix in the crab, egg white, 1/2 C. breadcrumbs, mayonnaise and lemon zest.

Step 4

Shape the mix into 8 cakes and place them on a lined up baking pan.

Step 5

Get a small mixing bowl: Stir in it 1/4 C. breadcrumbs, 1/2 tsp Cajun seasoning and 2 tsps oil. Press the mix into the crab cakes.

Step 6

Cook them in the oven for 22 min.

Step 7

To make the sauce: mayonnaise, sour cream, scallions, capers, mustard, relish and pepper. Serve it with the crab cakes.

Step 8

Get a mixing bowl: Whisk in it the

Step 9

Enjoy.

SPICY GINGER CAKE

Prep Time: 10 mins - **Total Time:** 45 mins

SERVINGS PER RECIPE: 12

NUTRITIONAL VALUE

Calories 387.0 , Fat 19.2g , Cholesterol 65.7mg , Sodium 257.2mg , Carbohydrates 50.8g , Protein 4.7g

INGREDIENTS

- 2 eggs
- 1/2 tsp ground nutmeg
- 3/4 C. dark brown sugar, packed
- 1/2 tsp baking soda
- 3/4 C. light molasses
- 1/2 tsp salt
- 3/4 C. butter, melted
- 1 C. boiling water
- 2 1/2 C. all-purpose flour
- 1 C. pecans, chopped
- 2 tsps ground ginger
- 1 1/2 tsps ground cinnamon
- 1/2 tsp ground cloves

DIRECTIONS

Step 1

Before you do anything, preheat the oven to 350 F.

Step 2

Get a large mixing bowl: Mix in it the eggs, brown sugar, molasses and melted butter.

Step 3

Add to it the rest of the Ingredients and combine them well. Add the boiling water and mix them well.

Step 4

Transfer the mix to a greased cake pan. Cook it in the oven for 36 min.

Step 5

Allow the cake to cool down completely then serve it.

Step 6

Enjoy.

HERBED CHICKEN AND CAJUN SKILLET

Prep Time: 20 mins **- Total Time:** 20 mins

SERVINGS PER RECIPE: 8

NUTRITIONAL VALUE

Calories 104.3 , Fat 2.6g , Cholesterol 24.6mg , Sodium 179.4mg , Carbohydrates 8.8g , Protein 12.5g

INGREDIENTS

- 3/4 lb skinless chicken breast, cubes
- 1/2 lb turkey kielbasa, slices
- 2 medium tomatoes, diced
- 1 medium onion, chopped
- minced fresh herbs
- 3 garlic cloves, minced
- 1 1/2 tsps Cajun seasoning
- 1 tbsp olive oil
- 1/2 tsp salt
- 1 medium green pepper, chopped
- 1/4 tsp pepper
- 1 medium sweet red pepper, chopped
- 1 tbsp cornstarch
- 1 medium yellow pepper, chopped
- 2 tbsp cold water
- 1 lb fresh mushrooms, sliced
- cooked spaghetti

DIRECTIONS

Step 1

Place a large pan over medium heat. Heat the oil in it. Cook in it the chicken, kielbasa, onion and garlic for 5 min.

Step 2

Stir in it the peppers, mushrooms, tomatoes, herbs, Cajun seasoning, salt and pepper. Let them cook for 8 min.

Step 3

Get a small mixing bowl: Whisk in it the cornstarch with water. Stir them into the pan. Cook them until they start boiling.

Step 4

Let them cook for 3 min. Serve your stir fry warm.

Step 5

Enjoy.

HANNAH'S MACARONI SALAD

Prep Time: 30 mins **- Total Time:** 40 mins

SERVINGS PER RECIPE: 20

NUTRITIONAL VALUE

Calories 225.0 , Fat 8.1g , Cholesterol 113.4mg , Sodium 684.1mg , Carbohydrates 20.5g , Protein 16.7g

INGREDIENTS

- 1 (16 oz.) boxes cooked macaroni noodles
- 1 tbsp Cajun seasoning
- 3 lbs medium unshelled shrimp
- 1 tbsp Accent seasoning
- 1 lb of real crabmeat
- 1 tbsp Mrs. Dash seasoning mix
- 1/4 C. finely chopped red onion

- 1 tsp onion powder
- 1 C. mayonnaise
- 1/2 C. sweet relish
- 1 C. sour cream
- 1/4 tsp cayenne pepper (optional)
- 1 tbsp spicy mustard
- 1 tsp garlic powder
- 1/2 C. butter or 1/2 C. margarine

DIRECTIONS

Step 1

Cook the macaroni by following the Directions on the package.

Step 2

Place a large pan over medium heat. Heat in it the butter. Cook in it the garlic for 1 min.

Step 3

Add the shrimp with Cajun seasoning then cook them for 4 min. Turn off the heat and stir in the crabmeat.

Step 4

Get a large mixing bowl: Toss in it the macaroni with onion and mayo and sour cream.

Step 5

Mix in the Onion powder, Garlic powder, Dash seasoning and Sweet Relish. Combine them well.

Step 6

Stir the creamy shrimp mix into the salad. Place it in the fridge for at least 2 h then serve it.

Step 7

Enjoy.

CAJUN CRAWFISH DIP

Prep Time: 15 mins - **Total Time:** 40 mins

SERVINGS PER RECIPE: 12

NUTRITIONAL VALUE

Calories 169.5 , Fat 10.7g , Cholesterol 67.2mg , Sodium 925.2mg , Carbohydrates 4.9g , Protein 13.5g

INGREDIENTS

- 2 garlic cloves, grated
- 1/2 C. scallion, thinly sliced, divided
- drained
- 1 tbsp butter
- 1/2 tsp kosher salt
- 1 lb crawfish tail
- 1/4 tsp black pepper, freshly ground, to taste 1 lb processed cheese, block
- 20 oz. diced tomatoes with green chilies,

DIRECTIONS

Step 1

Place a large pot over medium heat. Heat in it the butter. Cook in it the garlic with the white parts of scallions for 2 min.

Step 2

Stir in the crawfish and let them cook for 6 min. Transfer the mix to a large mixing bowl.

Step 3

Stir the tomato with cheese in the vacant pot. Cook them over medium heat for 2 to 3 min.

Step 4

Add to them the crawfish mixture with a pinch of salt and pepper. Cook them for 3 to 4 min. Serve your dip warm.

Step 5

Enjoy.

CAJUN KALE LUNCH BOX

Prep Time: 15 mins - **Total Time:** 35 mins

SERVINGS PER RECIPE: 2

NUTRITIONAL VALUE

Calories 749.3 , Fat 55.5g , Cholesterol 0.0mg , Sodium 3683.5mg , Carbohydrates 46.9g , Protein 29.7g

INGREDIENTS

- 2 bunches kale, teared
- 1 inch chunk gingerroot, finely chopped
- 1 (14 oz.) packages extra firm tofu
- 1 tbsp homemade Cajun seasoning
- 2 tsps Cajun seasoning
- 1 tbsp sea salt
- 1 C. carrot, matchsticks
- 1 tbsp cayenne pepper
- 2 eggs
- 1 tbsp paprika
- 4 C. water
- 1 tbsp garlic powder
- 1 tbsp vinegar, for poaching the egg
- 1 tbsp ground black pepper
- 1/4 C. olive oil
- 2 tsps onion powder
- 1 tbsp sesame oil
- 2 tsps oregano
- 3 tbsp tahini
- 2 tsps thyme
- 2 tbsp cider vinegar

DIRECTIONS

Step 1

Before you do anything, preheat the oven to 400 F.

Step 2

Place the tofu on a kitchen towel and cover it with another one. Let it rest for 16 min.

Step 3

Slice the tofu into long dices and toss them with 2 tsps of Cajun seasoning. Spread them on a lined up baking sheet.

Step 4

Cook the tofu dices in the oven for 24 min. Place it aside to cool down.

Step 5

Place a large saucepan of water over high heat. Heat it until it starts boiling. Blanch in it the kale for 3 min. Drain it and place it aside.

Step 6

Place a saucepan over medium heat. Pour in it 4 C. of water with 1 tbsp of vinegar. Heat it until it starts simmering.

Step 7

Crack each egg in a C. Use a wooden spoon to stir the water in around motion in one direction.

Step 8

Add to it 1 egg at a time while stirring all the time. Turn the heat off and put on the lid. Let the eggs cook for 4 to 5 min.

Step 9

Use a spoon to drain the poached eggs gently.

Step 10

Get a mixing bowl: Whisk in it the dressing Ingredients and place it aside.

Step 11

Place the kale and carrot on 2 serving plates then top each one with tofu. Drizzle over them 1/4 C. of dressing and a poached egg.

Step 12

Serve your breakfast plates right away.

Step 13

Enjoy.

CREOLE SCRAMBLED EGGS

Prep Time: 10 mins - **Total Time:** 30 mins

SERVINGS PER RECIPE: 2

NUTRITIONAL VALUE

Calories 476.6 , Fat 36.5g , Cholesterol 583.1mg , Sodium 755.4mg , Carbohydrates 9.9g , Protein 27.3g

INGREDIENTS

- 1 packages turkey sausage, sliced
- 6 large eggs, beaten
- 1/2 medium green pepper, chopped
- 1 tsp Cajun seasoning
- 1/2 C. shredded Monterey jack pepper cheese
- 2 tbsp olive oil
- 1/2 C. salsa
- 1 small red skin white potato, diced
- 1 small onion, chopped

DIRECTIONS

Step 1

Get a large mixing bowl: Mix in it the eggs with Cajun spice.

Step 2

Place a large pan over medium heat. Heat the olive oil in it. Cook in it the potato for 6 min.

Step 3

Stir in the onion with pepper and cook them for another 6 min. Stir in the sliced sausage and cook them for 3 min.

Step 4

Add the eggs mix and stir them well. Cook them for 3 to 4 minute while stirring it often.

Step 5

Stir the cheese into the scramble until it melts. Serve it warm with salsa.

Step 6

Enjoy.

MILD CAJUN EGGPLANT CASSEROLE

Prep Time: 30 mins - **Total Time:** 2 hr

SERVINGS PER RECIPE: 6

NUTRITIONAL VALUE

Calories 936.7 , Fat 61.1g , Cholesterol 218.7mg , Sodium 1874.2mg , Carbohydrates 58.3g , Protein 40.6g

INGREDIENTS

- 1 1/2 C. all-purpose flour
- 2 1/2 C. mild salsa
- 3 large eggs
- 1/2 lb tasso or 1/2 lb hot capocollo, chopped
- 1 C. milk
- 1/2 lb andouille sausages or 1/2 lb beef links, 4 C. breadcrumbs
- chopped
- 1 1/2 large eggplants, sliced
- 2 C. cheddar cheese, grated

- 8 tbsp olive oil
- 2 C. cheddar cheese, grated

DIRECTIONS

Step 1

Before you do anything, preheat the oven to 350 F.

Step 2

Get a large mixing bowl: Mix in it eggs with milk.

Step 3

Dust an eggplant slice with flour then coat it with milk mix and roll it in the breadcrumbs. Place it on a lined up baking pan.

Step 4

Repeat the process with the remaining Ingredients.

Step 5

Place a large pan over medium heat. Heat in it 2 tbsp of oil. Fry in it the eggplant slices for 4 min on each side.

Step 6

Lay half of the eggplant slices in a greased baking dish. Top it with 1 1/2 of salsa, all the ham and sausage. Sprinkle 1 1/2 C. of cheese over it.

Step 7

Lay the remaining eggplant slices on top then spread the remaining salsa over it followed by the remaining cheese.

Step 8

Place the pan in the oven and let it cook for 46 min. Serve it hot.

Step 9

Enjoy.

CREOLE ANY-NOODLES SALAD

Prep Time: 20 mins **- Total Time:** 40 mins

SERVINGS PER RECIPE: 10

NUTRITIONAL VALUE

Calories 212.2 , Fat 8.9g , Cholesterol 19.1mg , Sodium 633.2mg , Carbohydrates 29.3g , Protein 6.4g

INGREDIENTS

- 4 oz. chopped black olives
- 1 cans sliced mushrooms
- 3 stalks celery
- 1/2 red onion, sliced very thin
- 8 oz. Italian dressing
- 3 small tomatoes, chopped
- Salad Supreme dry seasoning
- 1 small bell pepper, sliced
- 8 oz. cooked noodles, any
- 15 oz. artichoke hearts
- salt and pepper
- 2 sliced cucumbers

DIRECTIONS

Step 1

Prepare the pasta by following the Directions on the package. Drain it.

Step 2

Get a large mixing bowl: Toss the pasta with the remaining Ingredients. Serve it right way.

Step 3

Enjoy.